GET SMART! HOW E-MAIL CAN MAKE OR BREAK YOUR CAREER AND YOUR ORGANIZATION

Mary Lynn Pulley & Jane Hilberry

Copyright © 2007 by Mary Lynn Pulley & Jane Hilberry

ISBN# 978-0-9797420-0-2

All rights reserved. No part of this book may be reproduced in any form by any electronic or mechanical means, including information storage and retrieval systems, without written permission from the authors.

Published by: Get Smart! Publishing, LLC

Art Direction, Design and Production: Jeannie Sheeks and Mike Reid

The authors wish to thank *The New Yorker* for generously granting permission to reprint the cartoons included here.

Table of Contents

Self Assessment 6

Impression Management 8

How E-Mail Can Make or Break Your Career 13

How E-Mail Can Make or Break Your Organization 19

The Petri Principle: What Makes E-Mail Different –
And More Dangerous 23

The Get Smart! Guidelines 31
   #1. Would You Want It to Appear in *The New York Times*? 34
   #2. Would You Say It Face to Face? 37
   #3. Is It Necessary? Or, About that Root Canal… 40
   #4. Does It Pass The Morale Test?
       Or, Who You Callin' Jelly Belly? 45
   #5. What's So Funny? 50
   #6. Is It Culturally Savvy?
       Or, Are You the Only One in a Tiger Suit? 53
   #7. What Would Your Lawyer Say? 58

Creating Leadership Presence 62

The Bottom Line 73

Acknowledgments

The authors would like to acknowledge their muses, Sage and Bill, who provided the insight and spirit of amusement that made this project a pleasure.

We would also like to thank all of our colleagues who for the past year have contributed support and examples of e-mail from their workplaces.

Please Note

All of the e-mail examples in this book (except the e-mail makeover example) are based on actual e-mail, and the stories are based on real situations. The particulars of the e-mail, individuals and organizations have been changed to protect the senders.

The authors are available to teach workshops on e-mail and a variety of other topics. Contact us at www.linkages.com

Praise for *Get Smart!*

"As Hilberry and Pulley point out, e-mail can take on a life of its own, draining our time, cutting into productivity, jeopardizing confidentiality and morale, and worse. *Get Smart! How E-Mail Can Make or Break Your Career and Your Organization* is a quick, humorous, immediately applicable read incorporating real-life examples, research data, and practical guidelines for e-mail usage. As an inveterate e-mail user, I highly recommend this delightful book."

– Richard F. Celeste, President, Colorado College, Former U.S. Ambassador to India

"We've all seen the occasionally humorous, and often disastrous, results of a poorly written e-mail. The authors provide clear and simple guidelines to avoid those pitfalls. I recommend it to corporate newbies and veterans alike."

– Jeffry L. Byrne, Vice President / General Manager, Air Products and Chemicals, Inc.

"*Get Smart!* is a unique contribution; it affords us an understanding of e-mail not simply as another form of technology-enabled communication, but linked intimately to leadership effectiveness. The authors offer real e-mail examples and practical advice to boost your e-mail intelligence, including an easy to complete self assessment and seven *Get Smart!* guidelines. Why will I recommend that leaders read *Get Smart!*? According to the authors, if we're not netiquette savvy, an errant e-mail could be the source of your leadership *e-railment!*"

– Nick Nissley, Ed.D., Executive Director, Leadership Development, The Banff Centre

Self Assessment

Check the most accurate response for each of the following statements. Record your score using the number in parenthesis ( ).

In the past month…

I have forwarded a chain e-mail or joke at work.
- ❏ More than once (1)   ❏ Maybe once (3)   ❏ Never (5)

I used Reply to All without considering whether everyone needed to read the e-mail.
- ❏ More than once (1)   ❏ Maybe once (3)   ❏ Never (5)

I have sent an e-mail for the sole purpose of raising a colleague's morale (your boss doesn't count!).
- ❏ More than once (5)   ❏ Maybe once (3)   ❏ Never (1)

I frequently send e-mail that is longer than two or three paragraphs.
- ❏ More than once (1)   ❏ Maybe once (3)   ❏ Never (5)

I have sent an e-mail with CONFIDENTIAL in the subject line.
- ❏ More than once (1)   ❏ Maybe once (3)   ❏ Never (5)

I have sent an e-mail with CONFIDENTIAL in the subject line to a distribution list of 15 or more people.
- ❏ More than once (-5)   ❏ Maybe once (-3)   ❏ Never (1)

I have sent an e-mail with the sole purpose of drawing attention to my own accomplishments.
- ❏ More than once (1)   ❏ Maybe once (3)   ❏ Never (5)

I have sent personal, intimate e-mail via my work account.
- ❏ More than once (1)   ❏ Maybe once (3)   ❏ Never (5)

Get Smart ! [Self Assessment]

I have sent, copied, or forwarded an e-mail to someone who didn't really need to receive it.
❏ More than once (1) ❏ Maybe once (3) ❏ Never (5)

I have sent an e-mail about my favorite political candidate to my department.
❏ More than once (1) ❏ Maybe once (3) ❏ Never (5)

I have checked an e-mail for misspellings, proper capitalization, and appropriate grammar.
❏ More than once (5) ❏ Maybe once (3) ❏ Never (1)

I have made a negative personal comment about someone else in an e-mail.
❏ More than once (1) ❏ Maybe once (3) ❏ Never (5)

I have forwarded an e-mail containing a negative comment about someone else.
❏ More than once (1) ❏ Maybe once (3) ❏ Never (5)

I have used text messaging abbreviations in an e-mail.
❏ More than once (1) ❏ Maybe once (3) ❏ Never (5)

I have sent an e-mail at 3 a.m. after drinking 3 or more whiskey sours.
❏ More than once (1) ❏ Maybe once (3) ❏ Never (5)

[Self Assessment

Total Score: Add up your 15 scores and record the total here _____

A score of:
3-19 = E-mail miscreant
20-35 = E-mail repeat offender
36-51 = E-mail pro
52-67 = E-mail superstar

Pulley and Hilberry

Impression Management
Chapter 1

Impression Management
Chapter 1

Have you, in the past few weeks, received an e-mail that irritated you, that made you angry, or made you cringe? Did it change your opinion of the person who sent it? Have you ever become so exasperated or offended by a colleague's e-mails that it undermined your respect for the person? When you see an e-mail that was sent by a particular person do you dread opening it—or automatically delete it without even bothering to read it?

More important, do you know if people are responding to your e-mails this way?

Even the most savvy of us make mistakes—and why wouldn't we? Most of us haven't received even the most basic training in how to use this medium that has sprung up and transformed the work landscape in an astonishingly short time. These pages will provide you with a set of Get Smart! Guidelines to use each time you send e-mail, to ensure that your communications create a positive impression and a positive impact in your organization.

This guide also provides a quick and easy way for organizations to cultivate collective e-mail intelligence.

E-mail mistakes made at any level of leadership can harm organizations. Whether it comes from the CEO or the newest hire, an e-mail construed as sexually harassing, for example, exposes the company to liability. In fact, the very democratic nature of e-mail makes it imperative that every member of an organization understand the implications and liabilities of using e-mail. Having clear guidelines and positive e-mail practices strengthens an organization's efficiency, performance, morale, and legal protections.

Often, employees simply don't know what their organization's e-mail norms and expectations are. Providing the Get Smart! Guidelines to everyone in your organization makes those norms clear and makes it easy for all members of your community to exercise e-mail intelligence.

Impression
Management
01

Get Smart! [Impression Management]

Will you miss those e-mail diatribes from chronically dissatisfied colleagues, those twice-a-day reports from your direct report about the state of her turtle's health, those uncomfortable jokes that send you scrambling for the Delete key? We think not.

Will you feel better knowing that the common understanding in your organization is that you don't conduct sensitive business via e-mail, that you don't circulate political e-mails or jokes, that you never, ever make comments about race, sex, or religion, and that you all honor the value of one another's time? We think you will.

"*On the Internet, nobody knows you're a dog.*"

© The New Yorker Collection 1993 Peter Steiner from cartoonbank.com. All Rights Reserved.

[Impression Management 01

Pulley and Hilberry

Goleman identified four aspects of emotional intelligence:

- **self-awareness**
  – how well do I know myself?

- **self-management**
  – how well can I control my impulses?

- **social awareness**
  – how well do I understand my environment and my impact on others?

- **social skills**
  – how well do I lead, communicate, and influence others?

e-Q

Daniel Goleman coined the term "emotional intelligence" to describe how the awareness of our own and others' emotions and awareness of the impact of our behavior on others is proving to be a more important indicator of success in the workplace than sheer intelligence (I.Q.) or technical skills.[1]

A new aspect of emotional intelligence is **e-mail intelligence:** are you aware of the impact that your e-mails are having on the people you're sending them to?

---

[1] Goleman, Daniel. (1995). *Emotional Intelligence: Why It Can Matter More Than IQ.* New York: Bantam.

# How E-mail Can Make or Break Your Career
Chapter 2

How E-mail Can Make or Break Your Career
Chapter 2

Now, more than at any time in the past, you can derail your career at light speed, simply by sending a hasty or ill-advised e-mail. A pattern of e-mails that are inappropriate, even if well intentioned, undermines your ability to lead. And because an estimated 84 billion e-mails are sent each day, the odds of making a mistake are great.[2]

Each e-mail you send—your modest contribution to the 84 billion daily tally—appears instantly in others' inboxes, and can be broadcast with a touch of the forward button. A single ill-advised communication can ruin a leader faster—exponentially faster—than it could before communication went electronic.

A 2006 survey shows that 26% of employers have fired employees for misusing e-mail.[3]

---

[2] Sandberg, Jared. (2006). "Employees Forsake Dreaded E-mail For the Beloved Phone." *The Wall Street Journal* Online, Sept. 26, 2006. www.online.wsj.com.

[3] American Management Association. (2006). "The 2006 Workplace E-Mail, Instant Messaging & Blog Survey: Bosses Battle Risk by Firing E-Mail, IM & Blog Violators." www.amanet.org.

And yet few of us have stopped to identify what makes e-mail communication disastrous or successful.

The way you use e-mail can make or break your career. If you communicate through e-mail at your work, you need this guide. It could save your career.

In today's workplace, e-mail is the most common form of communication. A survey of 546 leaders representing a wide array of industries showed that 98% of the respondents used e-mail daily.[4] Since so much business is now conducted electronically, and often remotely, we create the image others have of us largely through the way we present ourselves in e-mail. Most of us know how to behave in professional and social situations—we don't wear our sweats to the office, or talk loudly and non-stop through a dinner with clients, or put our personal issues on the agenda in department meetings.

In person, we've learned how to project a professional image, but many don't realize that image management is equally crucial in the realm of electronic communication. If you are the

[4] Pulley, M. L., Sessa, V. I., Fleenor, J. and Pohlmann, T. (2001). "E-Leadership: Separating the Reality from the Hype," *Leadership in Action*, 21 (4), 3-6.

person whose e-mail everyone dreads receiving, you might not even know it, because you can't actually see the others in the room rolling their eyes, edging away, or suddenly feeling an overwhelming need to refresh their drinks. Over e-mail, it is harder to gauge the impression you are making.

Imagine that you are a longtime employee of a firm that has a pragmatic, hard-working culture. A new V.P. named Mark joins the company, and during his first three months on the job, you (and everyone else in the organization) receive three, and only three, e-mails from him. Here are his messages:

> Can someone tell me the best place to get a Mercedes serviced? My new CL600 Coupe is giving me trouble.
>
> Can anyone recommend a luxury hotel for my upcoming stay in London?
>
> I have an extra high definition TV that I'm trying to sell – would anyone like to buy it?

What do you think of Mark? What assumptions would you make about his character from these communications? Would you trust him to put the company's interests above

e-Railment

The Center for Creative Leadership uses the word "derailment" to describe the career trajectory of professionals who have high potential but end up being sidelined, demoted, or fired. For over twenty years The Center for Creative Leadership has researched this concept by asking managers to think of someone in their organization who is successful – someone who is seen as effective and likely to continue to be promoted – and to think of someone else who derailed. Then they ask the managers questions like, "What were the fatal flaws that led to derailing?"

CCL's current research identifies five factors as the top reasons for derailment, listed in order of frequency:[5]

- Inability to change and adapt during a transition
- Problems with interpersonal relationships
- Failure to build and lead a team
- Failure to meet business objectives
- Too narrow business experience

We are seeing increasing instances of leaders who throw their career off track through e-mail. They e-rail. Colorado State Representative Michael Merrifield, Chair of the House Education Committee, sent an e-mail to the Senate Education Committee Chair in which he said there was a "special place in Hell" for charter school advocates. Two days after the e-mail was posted on a web site, Merrifield resigned as Chair of the House Education Committee. E-railment is the most highly accelerated form of derailment.

[5] Leslie, Jean Brittain and Van Velsor, Ellen. (1996). *A Look at Derailment Today: North America and Europe.* Greensboro, NC: The Center for Creative Leadership.

his own? After three months and three e-mails, you would have formed a definite impression, and it wouldn't be pretty. Mark forged his image—and e-railed his career—in exactly fifty words.

We construct an impression of ourselves each time we compose e-mail.

To excel in our careers, we need to be aware of how others perceive us, and we need to be intentional about managing the impressions we make. The ways to go wrong are myriad, and they lie at our fingertips each time we hit the Send button.

How E-mail Can Make or Break
Your Organization
Chapter 3

How E-mail Can Make or Break Your Organization
Chapter 3

How e-mail can make or break your organization 03

Did you know that a single e-mail can cause more damage to a company's stock in a single day than a poor quarterly earnings report?

A certain CEO sent an e-mail to his managers that focused on the fact that 8 a.m. and 5 p.m. were the busiest hours in the company parking lot:

> We are getting less than 40 hours of work from a large number of our K.C.-based EMPLOYEES. The parking lot is used at 8 a.m.; likewise at 5 p.m. As managers — you either do not know what your EMPLOYEES are doing; or you do not CARE. . .
>
> NEVER in my career have I allowed a team which worked for me to think they had a 40-hour job. I have allowed YOU to create a culture which is permitting this. NO LONGER.

The CEO threatened dire punishments, including closing the employee gym and laying off five percent of the workforce, if things did not change. The yardstick for success was that the parking lot would be full at 7:30 a.m. and 6:30 p.m. on weekdays and half full on Saturdays.

His e-mail made its way onto Yahoo (courtesy, perhaps, of an employee who didn't care to cultivate better parking habits) and within the day, thousands of people, including industry analysts and investors, had read this leader's rant. *The New York Times* picked up the story, and within three days, the value of the company stock plummeted 22%.

Leaders no longer have the questionable luxury of the private, internal rant. This CEO used e-mail as if it were an office memo typed and distributed via paper to employee mailboxes back in the 1980s. He didn't realize that once he hit Send, his communication was no longer private or internal. But he learned quickly. His message had the distinction of being one of the "most e-mailed articles" during April 2001.[6]

Now let us ask a rhetorical question: Was it more damaging to the company that the parking lot was not filled between

---

[6] Wong, Edward. (2001). "A Stinging Office Memo Boomerangs." *The New York Times* Online, Technology, April 5, 2001. www.nyt.com.

7:30 a.m. and 6:30 p.m. or that the CEO's inflammatory e-mail caused the company's stock price to fall from $44 to $34 in three days?

An analyst with Goldman Sachs posed the question, "Is this a CEO that investors are comfortable with?"[7] The entire company paid a steep price for this leader's poor impression management.

"I just think it undermines our organization's fiery rhetoric when you close your Internet postings with a smiley face."

© The New Yorker Collection 2006 Alex Gregory from cartoonbank.com. All Rights Reserved.

---

[7] Wong, Edward. (2001). "A Stinging Office Memo Boomerangs." *The New York Times* Online, Technology, April 5, 2001. www.nyt.com.

The Petri Principle: What Makes E-mail Different— and More Dangerous
Chapter 4

The Petri Principle: What Makes E-mail Different—and More Dangerous
Chapter 4

Bacteria flourish when they're in just the right environment. E-mail has created a completely new communication environment, a metaphorical petri dish that provides the precise conditions most favorable to certain kinds of e-mail errors. So what exactly is in the petri dish? What is it about e-mail that breeds error? The conditions that foster mistakes include the pressure to respond immediately, the illusion of impermanence, and the myth of confidentiality.

The Pressure to Respond Immediately

When a message appears in your inbox, how long do you feel you have to reply? How long can you wait before you imagine that the sender will assume that you are uninterested, unresponsive, or irresponsible? There is tremendous pressure in the current climate to respond instantly to all messages, a trend that is magnified by the use of BlackBerrys and Instant Messaging.

A university professor received an e-mail from a student on Tuesday afternoon, saying that he would have to miss the exam on Friday because he had to attend a cousin's wedding. The professor sent a reply mid-morning on Wednesday, and when she went into the office, discovered that the student and his mother had already lodged a complaint with the department that the professor was not accessible to students.

Stever Robbins, Executive Coach and CEO of the Stever Robbins Co., says he resists the pressure to respond instantly: "I intentionally slow down the conversation . . . I'll answer now but schedule the message to go out in a few days."[8] Allowing yourself a longer response period makes you less prone to make mistakes, partly because it creates time for reflection. Even if you simply pause for a few moments between composing and sending, you introduce a useful interval of reflection. You might think that it serves your organization best to keep a brisk pace in all communications, but this may be a false economy—depending on the nature of the business.

[The petri principle: what makes e-mail different— and more dangerous 04]

---

[8] Whitbourne, Kathryn. (2006.) "E-mail Excess." *Pink Magazine*, April/May 2006, 36.

Multi-Tasking

It was one of those days. Her daughter was home sick, but because of a crucial deadline Paula still had to go to work. She called every hour to check on her daughter. At the same time, an important but demanding client was sending a barrage of e-mails. In addition, Paula was trying to make arrangements with her travel agent for a meeting in Brussels in a few weeks. She was working as fast as she could so she could get home to her daughter.

The ping of the "New Mail" alert signaled yet another message from that annoying client. Paula read the message and decided to Forward it to a colleague who could take care of it for her, but first she added an editorial comment about the client: "Once again, she raises her scary head." Unfortunately, Paula hit Reply rather than Forward. The client was not amused. She immediately called Paula's boss. Both Paula and her boss had to go to great lengths to make reparations to the client over the coming weeks and months.

Two weeks later, Paula discovered that she had unwittingly booked herself into a presidential suite in Brussels that cost $3000 per night, a tad over the company travel budget. Her attempt to save time by doing everything at once proved costly in other ways.

Our brains are not built for multi-tasking. With any activity that requires a modicum of thought, the brain works on one task at a time, and what we view as multi-tasking actually constitutes a series of interruptions, whereby the brain has to shut down attention to one task in order to turn to another.

While we believe that we're efficiently juggling multiple tasks, our brains are actually toggling back and forth.[9] This toggling slows us down. Continuously moving between two or more tasks depletes our time and energy and interferes with our accuracy.

The most efficient way to work is to focus on one task at a time, setting aside specific blocks of time in which to attend to e-mail. A study of 1,000 employees at all organizational levels found that 55% open their e-mail either immediately or shortly after they hear that "ping." After being interrupted, the average amount of time it takes to return to the task is 25 minutes! These interruptions are estimated to consume 28% of our working day and cost the U.S. economy $588 billion per year.[10]

The bottom line: Turn off the "New Mail" alert. Don't attempt to answer e-mail while engaged in other work.

---

[9] Restak, Richard. (2003). *The New Brain: How the Modern Age is Rewiring Your Mind*. New York: Holtzbrinck Publishing, 54-59.

[10] Wallis, Claudia and Steptoe, Sonja. (2006). "Help! I've Lost My Focus." *Time Magazine* Online, January 10, 2006. www.time.com.

If an organization can afford a modest lag-time for e-mail responses, it may protect its reputation and avert lawsuits.

The Illusion of Impermanence

If you are in the habit of answering messages instantly, you may start to treat e-mail as if it were a conversation, responding off-the-cuff to whatever the sender says. But e-mail is not a passing conversation. That belief is an illusion.

A corporation that bestowed annual awards for outstanding performance gave an award one year to an employee who was widely known as a mediocre performer. A manager in another department received an e-mail from a direct report saying, "Can you believe that Joe won that award?" The manager sent back an e-mail saying simply, "No, I can't believe it." To the manager's astonishment, he was fired the next day. The IT staff had been monitoring e-mails and had reported the message to the manager's boss, who apparently did not think it innocuous.

You may think you are just bantering with a colleague or dashing off a quick reply that will vanish in the recipient's

Recycle Bin. But in fact, e-mail leaves a permanent trace. Corporations and organizations are now required by law to keep records of e-mail that can be called as evidence in trials.

Assume that anything you dash off in a message can and will be held against you.

The Myth of Confidentiality

One corporate manager suggested that her team conduct a discussion about a sensitive personnel issue over e-mail because it was "more private." This otherwise highly intelligent leader had not registered the fact that e-mail is the least private of all possible mediums. With a few keystrokes, an e-mail recipient can forward a message and reach more readers than the tabloids.

We have seen many instances in which someone sent an e-mail (one of them containing not-so-veiled criticism about the head of a department) to all the members of a distribution list, with a subject line announcing that the message was HIGHLY CONFIDENTIAL. Announcing that an e-mail is HIGHLY CONFIDENTIAL is a smart ploy if you want to increase your readership, but it is not an effective containment strategy.

Because business-related e-mail is not private, you should not use your work account for personal correspondence, except for the most mundane matters ("I'll be home in an hour"). Set up a personal account and use it for those messages in which you tell your best friend the details of last night's hot date.

Remember that everything you say via e-mail is public speech, and can become public record.

The Get Smart! Guidelines
Chapter 5

The Get Smart! Guidelines
Chapter 5

If you want to protect yourself and your organization from the ill effects of thoughtless e-mail, run quickly through this list before you hit Send. Post it by your computer. Recite it to yourself before you fall asleep. Chant it in your Buddhist meditation group. Soon you will have internalized the principles and will realize it as soon as you start to breach one of the rules.

When you check each step in the guide, it forces you to pause, even if only for a few seconds, before sending your message into cyberspace. Those few seconds of reflection time can be enough to avert an electronic disaster.

Ask yourself these questions before you send an e-mail:

#1. Would You Want It to Appear in *The New York Times*?

#2. Would You Say It Face to Face?

#3. Is It Necessary? Or, About that Root Canal...

#4. Does It Pass the Morale Test?
Or, Who You Callin' Jelly Belly?

#5. What's So Funny?

#6. Is it Culturally Savvy?
Or, Are You the Only One in a Tiger Suit?

#7 What Would Your Lawyer Say?

[The Get Smart! Guidelines]

#1. Would You Want It to Appear in *The New York Times*?

Get Smart! [The Get Smart! Guidelines]

#1. Would You Want It to Appear in *The New York Times*?

As previously noted, an unfortunate e-mail lapse can end up in *The New York Times*. Just to be safe, before you hit Send, think about whether it's o.k. with you if your e-mail is read by A) that person in your company who has always wanted to get you fired, B) your boss, C) the CEO, D) your grandmother, and E) the readership of *The New York Times*, print, online, and international editions.

[The Get Smart! Guidelines 05

"We can't go on like this, Herb. Last night I dreamed our e-mail made the National Enquirer."

© 2007 Carol Cable from cartoonbank.com. All Rights Reserved.

Pulley and Hilberry

What Were They Thinking?!

Bla, Bla, Bla

Dianna Abdala, a twenty-four-year-old law school graduate, was featured on CNN, ABC News' Nightline and in *The Wall Street Journal*. While any of us embarking on a new career might hope to be rocketed to fame, hers was not the sort to be envied: she was held up as an example of how to make oneself unemployable. Abdala, who was seeking a job in the Boston area, turned down a job offer with William Korman in an e-mail exchange. Some juicy tidbits are excerpted here:

> **Abdala:** The pay you are offering would neither fulfill me nor support the lifestyle I am living.
> **Korman:** ...you had two interviews, were offered and accepted the job (indeed, you had a definite start date).
> **Abdala:** A real lawyer would have put the contract into writing and not exercised any such reliance until he did so.
> **Korman:** This is a small legal community... Do you really want to start pissing off more experienced lawyers at this early stage of your career?
> **Abdala:** Bla bla bla.

Korman forwarded the exchange to a friend, and it circulated in the Boston legal community. It made its way to *The Boston Globe*, to *The International Herald Tribune*, and eventually showed up on the ABC News Nightline webpage with the headline "The Bla Bla Bla Heard 'Round the World."[11]

---

[11] Tappan, Jake. (2006). "The 'Bla Bla Bla Heard 'Round the World." ABC News Internet Ventures, Feb. 18, 2006. www.ABCnews.go.com/Nightline

[The Get Smart! Guidelines]

#2. Would You Say It Face to Face?

#2. Would You Say It Face to Face?

If you're sitting alone in your cubicle at 7 p.m. on a Friday night, or waking up at 3 a.m. after obsessing about what your co-worker said to you, it's easy to buy into the illusion that you are invisible. Writing e-mails when you're in an emotional state is like calling up your ex after drinking a six-pack of beer. There's something disinhibiting about the experience of writing e-mail.[12] No one is there to stop you. No one will say "What do you mean?" or "Why are you saying that?" or "Maybe you should get some sleep and we'll talk this over in the morning." No raised eyebrows or shocked expressions to tell you that perhaps you're taking the wrong tack.

One multi-million dollar financial company faced multiple lawsuits triggered by employee e-mails. A close inspection of the communications revealed that the vast majority of them had been sent between midnight and 5 a.m.

---

[12] John Suler describes the "Online Disinhibition Effect" in his hypertext book titled *The Psychology of Cyberspace*. www.rider.edu/~suler/psycyber/disinhibit.html

The safest approach is simply not to send e-mail that has any emotional charge. The best e-mail has an utterly neutral tone—unless it's a tone of unfeigned exuberance about your colleagues' successes. If a matter is sensitive, confidential, or potentially explosive, pick up the phone, knock on a door, or call a meeting. Work it out in person.

When sending e-mail, you need to learn to be your own audience, or to imagine your audience standing in front of you.

[The Get Smart! Guidelines 05

In fact, assemble them all in your imagination: every person on your receiver list. Would you stand up in front of them to express your views about the current president of the corporation? To complain that you didn't get the parking spot you rightfully deserve? Would you take the floor to ask for the name of a good proctologist?

If you wouldn't say it face to face, don't say it on e-mail.

Pulley and Hilberry

[The Get Smart! Guidelines]

#3. Is It Necessary? Or, About that Root Canal. . .

#3. Is It Necessary? Or, About that Root Canal. . .

We're all overwhelmed with e-mail. None of us wakes up hoping that we'll have just a few extra messages in our inbox this morning. Send your e-mail to the smallest number of people concerned. It's a matter of professional courtesy. You don't want to offend by excluding someone who ought to be informed or included in an e-mail, but the much more common offense is to clog the inboxes of uninterested bystanders. Honor your colleagues' time.

Resist the "Reply to All" reflex, and think about who really needs to hear your insight or whose action is required.

It saves more of the company's collective energy for you to take a second to choose the right recipient than for all twelve people to whom you automatically replied to delete your e-mail.

One man in an organization broadcast e-mails providing detailed accounts of his dental procedures to other employees.

Another person sent out involved accounts of her meetings with clients. Because the e-mails were so long, she would, from time to time, interject an encouraging message, such as "Keep reading—only 10 more minutes to go!"

Don't be that person.

Target your audience. Keep the message short. Make sure it's necessary.

e-Snowballs

E-mail can take on a life of its own. One controversial e-mail sent to an entire department or organization can cause a volley of Reply to All messages, so that before you know it, everyone on the list is doing a novel's worth of reading on the subject at hand. In one company, an e-mail was sent to all managers with the subject heading "The 12 Passenger Van," calling for a meeting about the company's transportation insurance. The e-mail became the vehicle for all manner of complaints, protests and expressions of dissatisfaction, and soon the e-snowball was rolling downhill faster than the 12 Passenger Van itself—and creating its own need for collision insurance.

If an e-snowball gets going, good leadership may require an intervention: call for a stop to the e-mails and set up a meeting to discuss the issues face to face.

Sometimes, however, stopping the rolling snowball may prove impossible. An employee of a global organization sent out an e-mail to a distribution list, worldwide, of about 20,000 people. The e-mail, written in Portugese, bore the subject line: Alguém

e-Snowballs (cont.)

pode responder a esta pergunta? (Can someone answer this question?) Soon people began to Reply to All with comments such as: "I don't understand—I don't speak Spanish." The snowball grew as many others Replied to All saying, "This isn't Spanish, it's Portugese." When the e-snowball began to clog company in-boxes worldwide, another round of Reply to All messages went out saying, "Don't Reply to All." Handwritten posters were put up in office buildings throughout the company warning employees not to reply to the Portugese e-mail. But this was a snowball on a mission: it couldn't be stopped. It ultimately caused the company's entire intranet system to shut down.

Bottom line: Don't automatically Reply to All!

[The Get Smart! Guidelines]

#4. Does It Pass the Morale Test?
   Or, Who You Callin' Jelly Belly?

e-Gotcha

A team can develop behaviors that undermine trust and performance, especially when the team is geographically dispersed and virtually all communication takes place through the phone or e-mail.

One team developed a creative way to kill all trust and morale. They called it "e-Gotcha." Whenever a team member made a mistake, another team member would point it out via e-mail to the entire team with the subject heading: e-Gotcha. It became a game to see how many mistakes could be tallied against each team member. Imagine how this would influence your motivation to fully engage with your team members—to open up, to take a risk, to try something creative—especially if you barely knew your fellow members.

This team became so dysfunctional that an outside consultant was called in. Needless to say, she could see that team members did not trust each other. Only when they agreed to stop sending "e-Gotcha's" and to call each other personally if sensitive issues arose did their performance improve.

#4. Does It Pass the Morale Test? Or, Who You Callin' Jelly Belly?

The now-former Chief of Police in Winter Haven, Florida, issued an e-mail to his department that went like this:

> Subject: Are You A Jelly Belly?
>
> As I look around the department I see a disconcerting number of us that appear physically challenged with obesity and/or a general lack of physical fitness. This is a tremendous concern to me because the literature, to say nothing of common sense, states that if you are obese and/or out of shape you are a predictable liability to yourself, your family, your partner, this department, the city of Winter Haven and the citizens of our city. So, take a good look at yourself.
>
> If you are unfit, do yourself and everyone else a favor. See a professional about a proper diet and a fitness training program, quit smoking, limit alcohol intake and start thinking self-pride, confidence and respectability. And stop making excuses for delaying what you know you should have been doing years ago . . .

Some residents of Winter Haven commented that they were not offended by the e-mail, but they were not the ones being fingered as Jelly Bellies. (The wife of a retired officer called the city to say she agreed with the Chief, but she may have had her own motives.)

If "self-pride, confidence and respectability" among the officers were the ex-Chief's aims, he chose a strange way to promote them. If he had set out to systematically demoralize his forces, he could not have done a better job. One long-time officer commented that he had "never seen. . . a morale problem like there is now."[13]

Make sure your e-mail passes the following Morale Test:

Ask yourself, "How would I feel if I received this e-mail?"

Would you feel worse about yourself (and the sender) than you did before you read it? If your e-mail doesn't pass the Morale Test, delete it, take a break (coffee and a doughnut, anyone?) and start over when you're in a better mood.

[13] Green, Merissa. (2006). "Haven Police Chief Sends Fat E-mail, Quits." *The Ledger* Online. October 24, 2006. www.theLedger.com.

By the way, two days after the Chief of Police issued his e-mail, he resigned. No amount of gym time could fix his image problem.

What Were They Thinking?!

What Shouting?!

Alain must have felt that an apology was in order after losing his cool in front of two co-workers.

Although he was contrite, Alain's apology did not lay the issue to rest, because he sent it not just to the two people who witnessed his outburst, but to the entire organization:

> I want to apologize for my rude, immature and inappropriate shouting earlier this afternoon.
>
> I am truly sorry.
> Alain Pfeister

He had now shouted the news of his bad behavior to everyone within electronic hearing distance.

[The Get Smart! Guidelines]

#5. What's So Funny?

#5. What's So Funny?

Few things seem as self-evidently normal to us as our sense of humor and our political views. Strangely, they are not always self-evident to other people.

Don't assume that others share your humor or your politics.

Don't forward jokes. Don't disseminate e-mail about political causes, speakers, events, or issues. Unless your employer is the Democratic National Committee or the Young Republicans, don't assume that you know your colleagues' political affiliations. And never assume that your co-workers share your religious views.

We hope it is not necessary to add that you should never send any e-mail with content, humorous or otherwise, that could possibly be construed (remember that person who's always wanted to get you fired) as biased in terms of race,

The Get Smart! Guidelines 05

gender, sexual orientation or religion—unless you're interested in finding a new job or sending your lawyer's children to college.

What Were They Thinking?!

I Apologize for My Incontinence

A man intending to correct a factual error in a report he had issued sent an e-mail apology to his co-workers. "I apologize for my incontinence," he wrote.

Thus he reassured his colleagues about his competence.

[The Get Smart! Guidelines]

#6. Is It Culturally Savvy? Or, Are You the Only One in a Tiger Suit?

#6. Is It Culturally Savvy? Or, Are You the Only One in a Tiger Suit?

A Director we know told a story about her first month in a new organization. It was October. She came from a company that loved to have fun and throw outrageous parties, so on Halloween, she simply assumed that everyone would come to work in costume, as they always had at her other job. She made a fabulous Tony the Tiger costume, complete with oversized head and striped tail. When she stepped into the office lobby, she saw that no one else was in costume. She stood silently in the elevator, watching through the eye holes of her big Tony the Tiger head, as her neatly clad co-workers pretended not to notice.

Every organization has a culture. The simplest definition of culture is that "it's the way we do things around here." Culture is manifested in the way people dress, how formally or informally they behave, what traditions and conventions they observe—and in almost every other aspect of institutional life. One predictor of success in leaders is their ability to read and adapt to organizational culture. Organizations seldom publish policy manuals that explain how to fit into the culture; new employees have to read the cues.

E-mail is an extension of your organization's culture, so pay attention to the culture's e-mail conventions and uses. How do people address each other in e-mail? Do they use titles or first names? How do they sign off? What level of diction do they use in their writing—is it casual or formal? What kinds of matters are discussed? Do they notify their bosses of their accomplishments, or would that be considered gauche?

Bill, a new sales manager, came from a company that had a very competitive culture. In that company it was perfectly o.k. to be self-promoting and brash—so long as you made your numbers. But the new organization emphasized collaboration. People did not brag about their success because the unstated belief—the cultural assumption—was that success speaks for itself. Bill sent an e-mail to the entire sales and marketing division, which included many different teams, with this subject heading and opening:

> **E-Mail**
>
> Subject: We're the BEST!
>
> The sales results for our team are AWESOME! We've reached 90% of our sales projections. By the end of the quarter I'm sure we'll exceed our goals and be the winning team!

If Bill had expressed his exuberance at a team meeting, or sent the e-mail only to his own team members, it might not have caused people to grumble. But those who were not on Bill's team were irritated and dismissive. Some of their teams were actually doing better than his. No one in the company had ever sent an e-mail like this before, and the mismatch between Bill's message and the organization's culture hurt his reputation.

Using e-mail in a way that deviates significantly from the norm will shape how others perceive you. Even if you've been with an organization for years, try comparing your own e-mail practices to others'. If you send ten e-mails for each one of your colleagues' or if you're the only one proclaiming your successes electronically, you may be inadvertently alienating yourself. If you are a new employee, err on the side of caution. Take some time to notice "the way people do things around here" before venturing out in your tiger suit.

Greetings and Sign-Offs

Two tricky moments in an e-mail are the greeting and the closing. Should an e-mail adhere to the traditional form of a business letter? Or is it an inherently more relaxed form of communication? The answer is that it depends—on the recipient and your organization.

Opening and closing phrases are in fact extremely important: they signal your respect for the recipient and your awareness of organizational norms. Generational differences may pertain here as well (some senior colleagues prefer that e-mails should always begin "Dear"). Organizational culture is crucial. In some academic institutions, faculty are always addressed as "Dr." or "Professor," while in others everyone, including students, addresses faculty by their first names. Notice what the prevailing practices are in your organization, and always keep your relationship to the recipient in mind. "Dear President Smith" may be appropriate in some cases; "Hi, Sam!" in others.

When in doubt, err on the formal side.

[The Get Smart! Guidelines]

#7. What Would Your Lawyer Say?

#7. What Would Your Lawyer Say?

Everything you write on your company's electronic system is the property of your company. Case closed.

This means that if your organization questions your performance and wants to review all e-mails that you've written over the past year, it has both the right and the means to do so. In fact, your organization has the right to review all of your e-mails even if your performance is not in question. You may dash off an e-mail or a text message in less than thirty seconds, but you've now created a digital record that will remain at your workplace at least as long as you do.

A 2006 study found that fifteen percent of organizations have been embroiled in lawsuits brought on by employee e-mail.

[The Get Smart! Guidelines 05

One in four companies have had employee e-mail subpoenaed.[14]

If an organization becomes involved in a lawsuit, information is discoverable. This means that once the suit is filed, both sides must discuss what electronic data they have and how they will provide it as evidence. Organizations involved in litigation are required to produce electronic information for their opponents in court. If they fail to produce what is often a massive amount of information they face stiff penalties.

Bottom line: the e-mails you write at work are not private. And because your company stores electronic correspondence, you cannot cover your tracks by pushing Delete.

---

[14] American Management Association. (2006). "The 2006 Workplace E-Mail, Instant Messaging & Blog Survey: Bosses Battle Risk by Firing E-Mail, IM & Blog Violators." www.amanet.org.

What Were They Thinking?!

Wonderful Memories

Spreading his own version of good cheer in the holiday season, Lynn, a retired Professor of Justice Studies, sent the entire campus the following response to the Chair's holiday wishes:

> To: The Campus
> Subject: Shawn
>
> It is not so much Shawn's holiday wishes that are the problem, but his pretense that he is a warm, friendly and loving person.
>
> In fact, he is a divisive and destructive person who has brought the Department into chaos. Can you imagine a Chair REFUSING to schedule an entire Department's fall schedule, forcing the Dean's Office to do it? This is not the act of a person who should be thanked or be given holiday wishes.
>
> Point made. I'll say no more.
>
> I have nothing but wonderful memories of my 36 years at this University and wish all of you the same.
>
> Lynn Jackson
> Professor Emeritus, Justice Studies

May all our holidays be filled with such wonderful memories!

Creating Leadership Presence
Chapter 6

Creating Leadership Presence
Chapter 6

The same features that make electronic communication treacherous make it powerful.

As a leader, you can reach and influence more people more quickly than anyone could have imagined a decade or two ago.

The democratic nature of e-mail makes it possible for executives to communicate quickly and economically with all members of an organization, not just those in their inner circle. It also makes it possible for members at any level of an organization to assume leadership. A smart leader will take advantage of the unique properties of e-mail to cultivate an informed and united organizational community.

Leading from Anywhere

The very nature of the Internet invites alternative ways to conceive of organizational connections. In contrast to the top-down model of leadership that has been dominant for decades, a model based on the metaphor of the organization as a web makes it clear that anyone in the system can have an impact on others. Leadership can come from above or below or from the middle—or, more accurately, from any strand of the web.[15]

One operations manager at a large hospital system averted a major crisis by mobilizing, through e-mail, co-workers throughout the organization. The hospital had switched to a new computer operating system which, unbeknownst to everyone, had created a glitch in equipment functioning that had serious ramifications for thousands of patients. When the operations manager discovered the problem, she realized that she needed immediately to mobilize her entire department to fix the computer glitch. She took the time to craft an e-mail that clearly stated what was wrong, what needed to happen, and the impact that this malfunction

---

[15] Van Velsor, Ellen and McCauley, Cynthia D. (2004). "Our View of Leadership Development." *The Center for Creative Leadership Handbook of Leadership Development*. Ed. Cynthia D. McCauley and Ellen Van Velsor. 2nd Edition. San Francisco: Jossey-Bass. 18-22.

would have on the hospital and the patients they served. She conveyed both the facts and the urgency of the situation, along with advance appreciation for the extra hours that would be required. Three hundred members of the department responded by coming in to work on the weekend, and they worked 24-7 to fix the problem.

Improving Morale

E-mail can powerfully influence both individual morale and the collective spirit of an organization. Wouldn't you feel differently about logging on to your computer in the morning if you thought your e-mail might bring you a word of praise or acknowledgment? Wouldn't it, in fact, make you feel better about your job? The now-former Police Chief of Winter Haven could easily have increased the "self-pride" of his force if he had chosen to praise rather than berate them. A simple personal message of congratulations can foster pride in a team or an individual.

E-mail can reinforce the morale of entire organizations as well. A leader can use e-mail to inform members of progress toward a goal (e.g. fundraising), of outstanding performance (e.g. stock prices), or of other victories (positive media coverage, industry awards, etc.). Such messages constitute positive impression management for the organization as a whole: we all prefer to be part of a winning enterprise.

But even—or perhaps especially—when an organization is going through rough waters, regular communication from top leaders can keep members informed of the organizational strategy, foster a sense of unity of purpose and, perhaps most important, reassure members that someone is in fact awake at the helm.

Leading through Change

One of the most powerful moves a leader can make when an organization is going through change is simply to stay in view. At one university, it fell to the Director of Security to explain and enforce a new parking policy. For the first time, students, staff and faculty had to pay for their parking and had to park in assigned lots. No one was overjoyed at the prospect, to put it nicely.

The Director of Security dubbed himself "The Parking Meister" and sent out a steady series of e-mails that educated the community about the new policies. He also managed, though humor, to diffuse tensions.

Right now you may be thinking, "But we're not supposed to use humor in e-mail! You said so yourself!!" That's true, and while we would be loathe to encourage any breaking of our well-crafted rules, in this case the humor worked, probably because the Parking Meister made himself, rather than others, the target of his jokes.

The Director of Security literally walked everyone through the transition: in response to complaints that people would have to walk too far from their parking lots to their buildings, the Parking Meister wrote,

> **E-Mail**
> I am sure that you heard of the movie "Dead Man Walking." Well, you can call this next scenario "Old Man Walking." I walked the campus just to get an idea of how long it takes to get from certain parking lots to certain buildings.

He detailed the times of his walks—2:17:22 minutes to walk

from Lot A to Building X. 1:43:49 minutes from Lot B to Building Y, etc.

It was hard to get worked up about those distances.

The Parking Meister maintained his leadership presence throughout the transition by sending daily e-mails as the new policies went into effect:

> **E-Mail**
>
> Well, looking over the campus parking lots today, I think congratulations are in order. You are all doing very well, except for a few of you that haven't registered your vehicles yet. So, one more time, if you want to park on campus, you must register with Campus Security. The next step in the parking process will be "Tickets, Boots, and Tow Trucks, OH MY!" A few of you are registered but need to park in the correct lot. But I understand that it all takes time getting used to, so that's why no tickets so far.
>
> As an instructor in Parking 101, I give you all a B plus.

The next day the university community received an A minus.

The Parking Meister earned an A plus for creative leadership.

Keeping Communication Open

Electronic communication makes it possible for a leader to establish presence quickly in a global organization. In one organization, the new CEO's first action was an electronic act: he sent an e-mail to every employee with a realistic, upbeat message about the organization's future. He outlined strategic priorities. And he made it clear that two-way communication was crucial to his leadership.

> **E-Mail**
>
> Over the next three months, I plan to visit all five of our campuses with a primary goal in mind: listening carefully and learning how we can have even more impact in the future. I want to hear from you about what we do well and what we can do better. Your collaboration and superb work bring the company's mission to life, and your honesty and feedback will always be appreciated and valued.

This e-mail beautifully illustrates the power of positive impression management. In a single e-mail, the CEO established his leadership style and presence. His communication immediately gave employees confidence in his ability to steer the organization.

Increasingly many top executives are using other forms of electronic communication, such as blogs, to give interested parties a window into a leader's mind.

A growing number of CEOs use blogs to communicate their thoughts about safety concerns, company direction, the competition, issues related to globalization, and similar matters.

Please note here that you must be every bit as careful in posting to a blog as you are in sending e-mail. Even personal blogs have been used to call employees into question.

One President of a private college created a public blog to post his thoughts and respond to readers, signaling the fact that he is available and responsive to a wide community of students, parents, faculty, and interested members of the public.

After the Virginia Tech shootings, in a blog titled "Sanctury. Enter at Your Own Risk," the President reflected that

> This sanctuary, where we join in a focused effort at teaching and learning...can be invaded by the sharp, all-too-frequent outbreaks of savage violence that seem to plague our society.

The President described how his campus had expressed its sadness and solidarity with the Virginia Tech community and reported that his key administrators met to review what to do on the campus should it be confronted by some unimagined random act of violence.

One reader recommended a book about how to prepare for violent events, and the President thanked him on the blog for the suggestion. One parent requested that he "keep sending the messages of safety and support."

By posting a blog and responding to messages, the President managed both to create a forum for two-way communication and to reassure the community that the college was addressing potential threats.

e-Mail Etiquette

The telephone has been around long enough that common courtesies have evolved. Most people know that slamming the phone down in someone's ear without saying goodbye is rude. Such courtesies are still evolving with e-mail. Here are some that we recommend:

- Use a subject heading that reflects the content of the message.
- Be concise. If you can say it in three words, say it in three words. Limit yourself, at most, to a few short paragraphs.
- State your request clearly at the outset: what action or response do you require?
- Do not ever say anything negative about a person. Do not repeat or forward someone else's negative comment.
- Use proper spelling, grammar, and punctuation.
- Use italics or bold face (sparingly) to emphasize a point. Don't capitalize: IT'S JUST LIKE SHOUTING.
- Don't forward chain letters, jokes, or political messages.
- Don't format daily communication with colored text and background colors or images. It looks unprofessional, is hard to read, and makes replying difficult.
- Keep your electronic signature to five lines or less.
- Do not push the Send button between midnight and 5:00 a.m. Wait until the sober light of morning to send any of your midnight brainchildren.
- Use Reply to All only when every single person on the list needs the information.
- Delete virus warnings – they're often hoaxes.
- If your organizational e-mail protocols are not clear, ask for clarification or initiate a conversation about it.

If you want to learn more about e-mail etiquette, search "Netiquette" on the Web. Netiquette seeks to delineate respectful communication practices for Internet exchanges. E-mail protocols change, and many sites are devoted to detailing the best current practices.

The Bottom Line
Chapter 7

The Bottom Line
Chapter 7

Because e-mail is new and unlike other, more familiar forms of communication, it's easy to make mistakes.

Having read our e-mail horror stories and taken in our strict Get Smart! guidelines, you may tremble to ever send an e-mail again. In fact, we have all made—and, in truth, will probably continue to make—mistakes in our e-mail practices. But we hope to have steered you away from some of the most egregious, and expensive, types of errors.

If you bear in mind a few principles, you can make a positive, powerful impression in your electronic communications.

- Every time someone reads your e-mail, they form an impression of you. Make a conscious choice about the kind of image you convey.

- Every e-mail you send makes a demand on the recipient. Be considerate of others' time and attention.

- Every e-mail you send (if read!) will evoke some response in the recipient. Make it a positive response.

Take a minute to imagine how the recipient might react, and change anything that could possibly result in misinterpretation, insult, or loss of morale.

Think, for a minute, of someone whom you admire both professionally and personally. Are we right that this person treats you and others graciously? Do you feel acknowledged and respected in this person's presence? Wouldn't you hope that others view you the same way?

Writing e-mail is a creative act. If you approach it consciously, you can shape a positive electronic presence, which will, very likely, make others more receptive to your inquiries, requests, or direction. All of which makes your life, and the life of your organization, run more smoothly.

E-Mail Makeover

Before

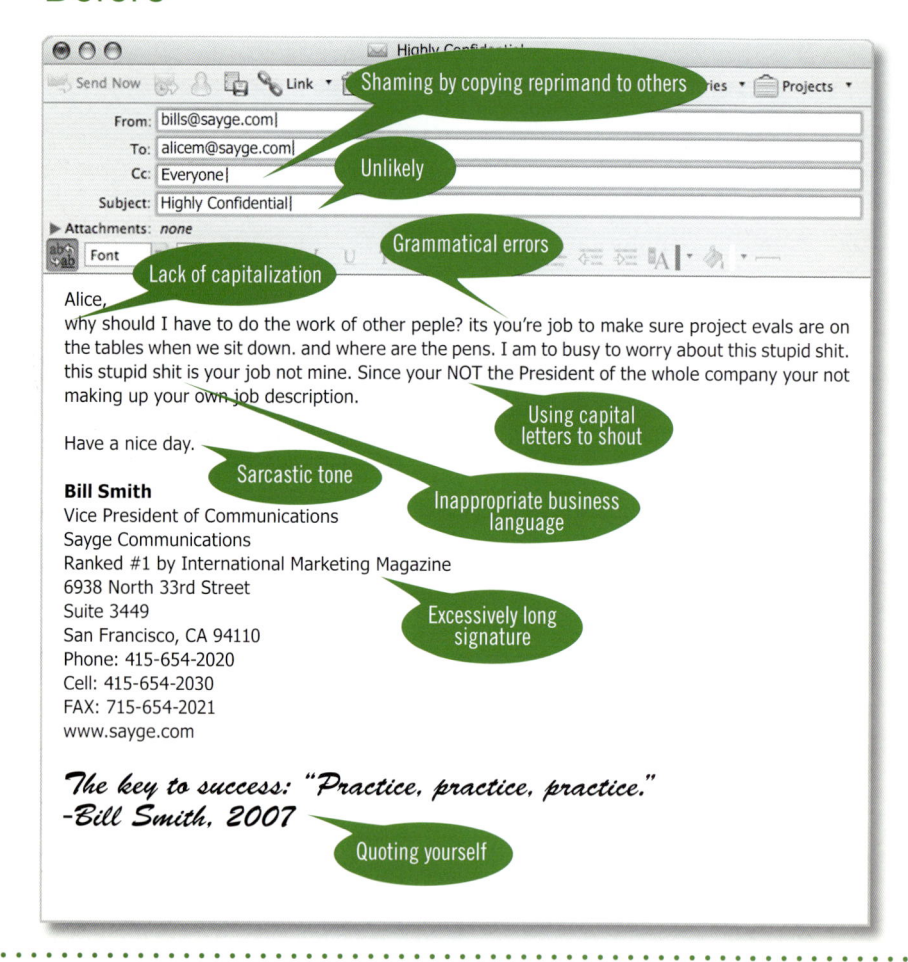

Annotations:
- Shaming by copying reprimand to others
- Unlikely
- Grammatical errors
- Lack of capitalization
- Using capital letters to shout
- Sarcastic tone
- Inappropriate business language
- Excessively long signature
- Quoting yourself

From: bills@sayge.com
To: alicem@sayge.com
Cc: Everyone
Subject: Highly Confidential
Attachments: none

Alice,
why should I have to do the work of other peple? its you're job to make sure project evals are on the tables when we sit down. and where are the pens. I am to busy to worry about this stupid shit. this stupid shit is your job not mine. Since your NOT the President of the whole company your not making up your own job description.

Have a nice day.

Bill Smith
Vice President of Communications
Sayge Communications
Ranked #1 by International Marketing Magazine
6938 North 33rd Street
Suite 3449
San Francisco, CA 94110
Phone: 415-654-2020
Cell: 415-654-2030
FAX: 715-654-2021
www.sayge.com

The key to success: "Practice, practice, practice."
-Bill Smith, 2007

Get Smart! [E-Mail Makeover]

After

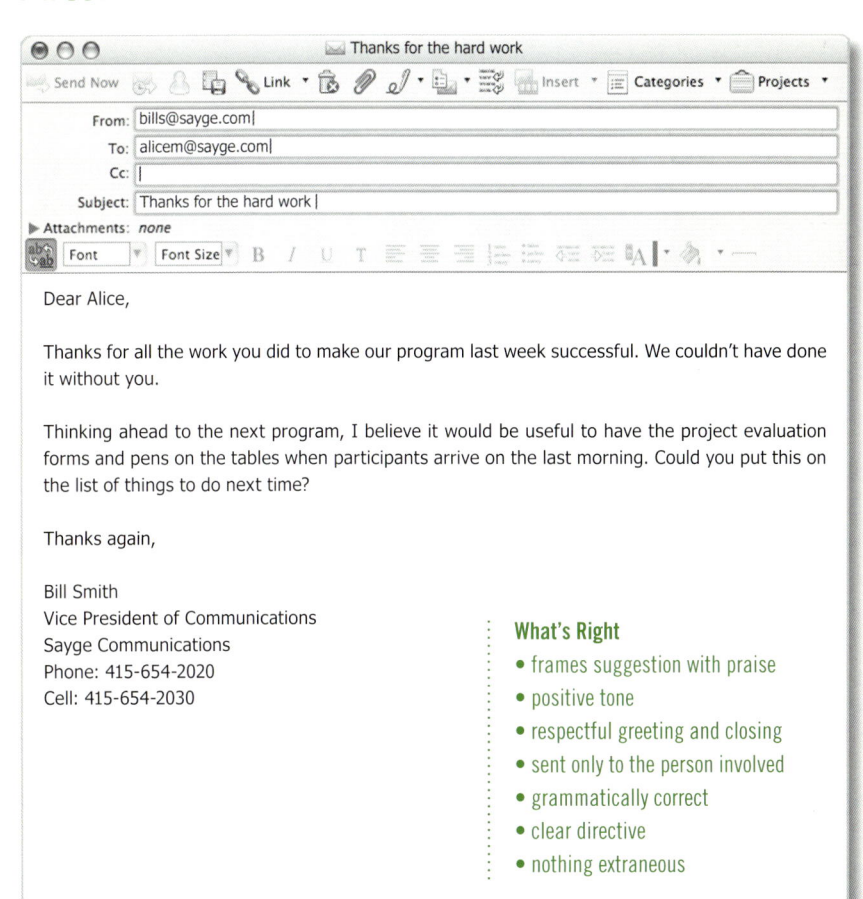

Subject: Thanks for the hard work

From: bills@sayge.com
To: alicem@sayge.com
Cc:
Subject: Thanks for the hard work
Attachments: none

Dear Alice,

Thanks for all the work you did to make our program last week successful. We couldn't have done it without you.

Thinking ahead to the next program, I believe it would be useful to have the project evaluation forms and pens on the tables when participants arrive on the last morning. Could you put this on the list of things to do next time?

Thanks again,

Bill Smith
Vice President of Communications
Sayge Communications
Phone: 415-654-2020
Cell: 415-654-2030

What's Right
- frames suggestion with praise
- positive tone
- respectful greeting and closing
- sent only to the person involved
- grammatically correct
- clear directive
- nothing extraneous

About the Authors

Mary Lynn Pulley is the President of Linkages Workplace Consulting®, LLC. In this capacity she provides executive coaching and leadership development to a variety of clients. Mary Lynn is a former Enterprise Associate at the Center for Creative Leadership. As a member of the Center's Research & Innovation Group, she focused on the impact of technology on leadership. She is the author of numerous publications, including *Losing Your Job – Reclaiming Your Soul: Stories of Resilience, Renewal, and Hope*, and has been quoted in *Fortune Magazine*, *TIME-Asia*, and *Leader to Leader*. She holds an M.A. in Counseling Psychology from the University of North Carolina at Chapel Hill and an Ed.D. in Human and Organizational Development from Vanderbilt University.

About the Authors

Jane Hilberry is a Professor of English at Colorado College, where she has taught Creative Writing for nearly twenty years. Jane offers workshops to foster powerful expression among leaders. For the past five years, she has served as a faculty member for the "Art of the Executive Leader" program in Leadership Development at the Banff Centre in Canada. Jane has published two books, most recently a volume of poetry titled *Body Painting*, which won the Colorado Book Award for Poetry. Her other honors include a Colorado Council on the Arts Recognition Award for Poetry and a Colorado Endowment for the Humanities Research Award. Jane graduated Phi Beta Kappa from Oberlin College and received her M.A. and Ph.D. in Creative Writing and Literature from Indiana University.